KU-453-902

THIRD
SPACE

A Forest of Unified Violence

Anette Appaduray

Listen to the cicada
buzzing loudly in the humid night

while the crickets, grasshoppers, katydids
shout odes of love and loss,

frogs yelp their worries
from wet hiding places.

When the gathered, tender cries
of the forest's underbelly

work in solitude and unison,
each with unique and purified purpose,

a kind of violence is born.
Between the trees and the branches and the bramble

an orchestra of darkness
wraps the forest

whole. Are you listening?
The night deepens.

[3]

A Sestina to Myself

Kathleen Wenaden

I sent to myself those moon-blue letters
of my folded origami lives
tucked tight into my body,
those creased words and fragments
holding tight on to my edges
and always ending with blessings.

The nun-aunty who sent soft white blessings –
on flat blue airmail letters
spindly writing up to the edges.
Speaking of all the lives
she touched, and the bright fragments
of family news she kept inside her body.

She spoke of her body,
the other nun-aunty of loud red blessings
and a life stuffed full of fragments.
Travels to Egypt, spoke her letters
In language, instructions for our lives,
Yet she helped to fill in my edges.

My father had such slanted edges,
held too much tight inside his body.
He spoke of those Sri Lankan lives,
the ones held up as blessings.
Still they came, those letters,
Yet all he passed to me was fragments.

I hold those milk-white fragments,
fist closed, tight along my edges.
Bowed down with all these letters
in the deep holes of my body.
Kept in the stillness of blessing
And in my other origami lives.

Today I call out these othered lives
and open up the fragments,
piece together these blessings.
I open up this bright new body
as once I welcomed those letters.

So I will gather all these lives, written right up into my edges,
Those fragments found in darkness, deep, deep inside my body.
Filled up with blessings and spoken aloud in those letters.

Asghari and the Tree of Destiny, 1933

Laila Sumpton

She cantered into the village
with a satchel full of condoms –
square wrapped destinies,
the rubbery power of no.

Family trees quivered
at her invasion, and the land,
tired at being divided and divided
till there was no space to grow,

uttered a sigh. Finally, someone
and something to battle hunger,
give village women a break
from endless cycles of birthing.

No men allowed at the meeting.
The plan was simple – gather women,
describe, persuade, distribute,
then canter back to Lahore

for the dinner she was hosting.
She finished her speech, glad
she remembered to speak slower,
but they just stared; some giggled.

The revolution had not landed –
she would have to demonstrate –
and cursed her lack of props.
She broke a stick, showed the ladies

how easy it was to apply.
Suddenly there were smiles, nods,
general enthusiasm,
an empty satchel, canter home.

Months later she returned,
keen to see how her gifts,
her magic packets
had empowered these ladies.

They sat under the meeting tree,
bellies blooming and defiant:
we did what you asked;
your covers do not work. See –

we all put them on the tree
like you showed us.

Apple Chutney

Jaweerya Mohammad

the row of crab apple trees amongst apartments,
grandma's crooked bony finger
behind a window screen,
pointing at us to pluck the ones coloured like sunrise.

the tiny apples, marbles,
their speared stems with leaves
smushed on the floor, clustered on branches.

we make spilling baskets
by folding over the corners of our kameez,
fingers tearing stolen fruit,
weaving away worms, wasps and bees.

cousins dare and wince;
our teeth sink into sour,
the ringing laughter after
half-eaten cores pelt our backs,
shoulder-blades sting, sweating,
we stumble inside splattered in apple sauce.

the mothers scold, rush, rinse,
pour vinegar and spice,
boil until the fruit's thin skin blisters
and breaks,
mashing into a spread...

this is how my memories meander,
how wistfulness saunters in,
nostalgia nestles in long after
like the jarring of crab apples –

fruit once biting and tart,
the lid only twisting open
when its contents are cool, sweet
enough to lull on my tongue.

Beginning of the End

Nawshin Flora

Blooming hibiscus, moonless sky, laboured breaths,
your hand in mine.
The sirens of death are humming – is that a sign?
Ma, tell me, how do I prepare for your funeral?
Can I take my time and say goodbye to all the cells that
     construct your body?
Do you think god would grant me that much time?
Tell me, how do you not fall off the cliff
when you are standing on the edges
of the beginning of the end?

I see you die a little every day:
Your cheeks have now become paler,
your hands shake when they reach for your teacup.
Your smile doesn't reach your eyes, and in that miniscule
     moment
grief possess my body and dips my hand into the river where
my voice can't reach yours.
It makes me want to gnaw the skin of the deceitful god.
There are nights when you can't sleep,
and I blame the stars for being so faithless.

Your body – proof that death exists.

When I place my hand on the curves of your belly,

taking in your scent, locking it to my memory,

I can see your eyelids fluttering, while your hand struggles to
    join mine.

Grief finds me every day, taking me to the fringes of nothingness,

collapsing, entangled, making a hole in the core of my body.

A poem is the culmination of a tragedy.

I have run out of metaphors now, Ma.

I don't know how to let go of you. I want to say I love you,

but I know there can never be enough times I could say it to you

and make time stop and deceive death so its hands can't reach
    you.

I want to say I am sorry because I haven't been kind to you, but

It will never be enough to bring back the time where I haven't
    learned to hurt you yet.

But I am sorry, and I love you, Ma.

You had a life before me, but my life began with you.

And it will end with you.

Body/Border

After the artwork 'Looking Glass' by Janna Ajmal

Ilisha Thiru Purcell

There are no borders here
except the one I hold in my teeth.

The hinge of your arm to chest
is the horizon is the mountain
is the wedge of moon

two syllables, bo/
bor – bo: open
lips, pop – open
space
fill it with air
you and I become the sand
or the other way around.

The sunset drips
down the canvas
that is your head against mine.
When you speak
purple wax falls
and I write my name with it.

There's no border here
except the one I try to swallow.

The hinge of your arm to chest
is the horizon is the mountain
is the wedge of moon

bor: closed
sound of the r, a rolling, a chew-
ing over. How large is it in the mouth?
Tell me, what is the difference between
a boundary and a border?
I let you draw around me in the sand.

I can't see a border from here
only that hinge of your arm to chest
is the horizon is the mountain
is the moon.

Brief Essay on

Intergenerational Trauma

Sneha Subramanian Kanta

The music won't be interrupted, not like when you try to talk about family history. This teaches us about the quality of silence in rooms where your words will not be welcome because they are an utterance of truth. People make it about it being your truth. The supple skin on your forearms leading unto your shoulders, slightly curved from sitting on the laptop all day, has another story to tell. The body changes in accord with the carrying of years. It differs in the shape aligning with what has not been put to shape. The physiotherapist gives you an exercise which resembles flapping your shoulders inwards and outwards, like a bird would toss rainwater from wings and plumage. This will be a good way to guide the shoulders into place. Do you use an ergonomic workspace? You need your body to put the body back into place. You don't need anyone else's unremembering.

Bright Thread

Moniza Alvi

One aunt, two aunts
            three aunts gone
      my uncles gone
and my father gone.
      It's my English mother
            who holds the thread
      always keen to connect
            with distant Pakistan.

      Now it's clear
that she who made her home
            in a land so far from home
is herself a country
      to which I'll hold the thread.

            I'll practise now.

      This is the thread.
            This is the eye of the needle.

Brown Girl Duplex

After Jericho Brown

Kari Pindoria

I was born with too much wanting.
Taught that every daughter is a stolen son.

        Every daughter is her mother's leftovers:
        jewellery, childhood stories, Swahili words.

I know the Swahili word for plate but not love.
I'm always the hungriest at night.

        Nights hungry for rum & a Skepta verse.
        I spit out brown-girl curfew, gossip from aunties.

Gossip spits out like tobacco on concrete.
Generations of shame, a connect-the-dots.

        Walls dotted with generations of women
        Not smiling in their wedding photos.

I'll be smiling at my wedding like a crime
For being born with too much wanting.

Chorizo from the Old Country

Selma Carvalho

we arrive nowhere, curved mouth of road, squeezed
into cul-de-sac, slender and slump-shouldered.
serrated light of lamp, faint dusting of snow
seaming the street, cold seeping into bone.
on the verge, he meets us, old fabled folk
unsure, ungainly, moustachioed.
links in hand, links to our sunken past,
he hands them over.
we leave him behind, rear-mirrored, receding,
halved, quartered, remaindered, standing small, smaller now,
only a speck, forgotten.
we drive home, the smell of chorizo from the old country,
gut-sheathed, garlic-sweated, filling up our car.
we rise next morning, the air fire, our breath a smokescreen.
we cry over nothing at all.

Dad/Drama Queen

Jayant Kashyap

the boys are learning   to fish.
the tap-water   running   sings itself   into a bucket.
the night breathes in over 19,500 languages/   tongues.
the rivers have lost   the boats/   hands.
the social media are a soft porn   of everything.
~~the ink is mud-riddled~~   ~~blood.~~
the Ganges shark, the few, have thought of a protest.
the AQIs around   the nation have their own deliberations.[1]
the people talk about *today's weak plastic*   *buckets.*
the new children are learning acid-words/   words that burn.
the youth are getting rid of paper   money.
the fathers   are infatuated with remotes;
                                            infuriated with the boys.

the girls   ready to marry   talk of china.
            the porcelain readies itself   to break.
the oceans are the largest sewers;   blue/green/grey.
~~the public almost know how~~   ~~change dot org works.~~
the news channels are hopelessly in love   with lies; white/grey.
the snowcapped hills look *rather dashing* in incoherent shades of black.

---

1 *AQIs*: Air Quality Index. Used for reporting daily air quality; tells how clean/polluted air is, and notes associated health effects.

the sweet glycerine   oddly substitutes tears in plays   of salt.
the mothers have a penchant for   everything.
the leaves always work in the right vein.
the govt would rather loan money to the rich − to them,

the slums are sluts (noun, *off.*).

~~the owls love eating~~   ~~poisoned mice.~~
the ostriches have buried their head in the sand; their *arses*

to the sun.

~~the A4-size paper is too thick~~   ~~to be written upon.~~
the white chocolate   is only drained-out

dark chocolate.

the pigeons are better than the chickens/   the squirrels;

soft/   meat.

the earth is probably almost   ready   to stop;

my lungs are heavy.

the statues of the gods are cold   bodies.
~~the father says he's ready~~   ~~to change~~   ~~for a heart bypass.~~
the blue apron has a sweet   *texture*; he   kisses it.
~~the lives of many aren't so difficult~~

~~but they make it.~~

'Dad/Drama-Queen' is a conventional, sometimes satirical take on what fathers (sometimes) do at homes. Without trying to be offensive, the lines in the poem are parts of imagined (and sometimes unimagined) comments and monologues, and serve to present an outlook on life and the world.

Draw It on a Map

For my Pakistani cousins

A.A. Malik

Once, they asked me to draw it on a map.   I couldn't.
On a map, you see, it doesn't exist.
It only exists in the brown, smoothly wrinkled skin of the buffalo,
white-whiskered and frothy-mouthed.
A double curl of concrete horns protruding from its head,
solid in its massive frame, it stands
within the centre of this place,
and around it spin fields and swings and skies.

Its skies are not the same skies as this ersatz sky overhead, this
oppressive sky, this
peppered wool sky, which hangs like a canopy over worker ants.
In that other sky the birds are free
to choose
how to fly, where to rest. Clocks are a fable. A place where
placenta, that once nourished animal babies,
is flung up high amidst the branches of trees to sustain free birds.

That place doesn't exist on a map. It barely exists outside of itself.
To reach it, people give directions to 'turn left at the knotted tree',
and 'then right, past Chota Hamid's kothi',
past the field of grazing cows, past the qurrah-carrying women
    (marvel at the ones not using an uno).

That place where we gathered five paisa
to buy sweets from the only village shop.
It's where we walked in the day together through luminous
yellow-flower fields
    (also, at night for pre-bedtime wees).
Past houses with crumbling, aged façades,
past children with dirty bare feet and kohl-ringed eyes,
past the graveyard
    (don't look at it, just walk, recite quickly, walk quicker, nearly
    there, OK, breathe).

That place where we sat for hours endlessly
shelling sunflower seeds,
badger-striped, salty shells
yielding miniscule, yet coveted prizes from within,
and we talked and laughed and grew.

That place,
beautiful in the early morning,
nostalgic at sunset and
like Shaytaan's home when the sun was at its zenith.
That place where the girls made fabric dolls and I marvelled
at their young ingenuity and, despite my plastic Barbie at home,
I envied their toys.

That place was half of my heart as a child.

That place I haven't felt for years.

That place, I can't get to now. Even if I were to drive through borders that were once open,

that place, I can't find, because it doesn't exist on a map, you see.

Now,   it just doesn't exist.

Glossary

Chota: Small/younger

Kothi: Mansion

Qurrah : Clay pots used to carry and store water

Uno: Torus made of fabric which sits under the clay pots (used both when pots are resting and also on top of heads to keep the qurrah in place when walking)

Paisa: Pakistani coin

Shaytaan: The Devil

Eurydice's Wardrobe

Z.R. Ghani

I walk in, supposing the storm nestles
in the pockets of these limp garments
without bodies to transport them,
give them purpose. For a moment,
I'm among strangers at a funeral,
troubled by their impermanence.

These clothes once held me like bottles
keep their poison or cure; I'm not sure:
the 90s dungarees, the demure lengha
I wore to every wedding, a denim jacket.
The door slams and locks, I must go.
Eurydice, the storm said, *you mustn't
look back when you leave the underworld.*

What is my maternity gown doing in here,
with its stitches slipping out of their tunnels,
tossing their prison on the floor? Polka dots
fall softly like forlorn full stops from my red
prom dress. Inside a hatbox without a lid
is a jaggery-hued fawn curled up. Her shaky
eyes. Her tears a sprinkling of snow or sugar.
Her moth-eaten fur. All too familiar.

My eyes hurt from the vulgarity of daylight.
Give me back the darknesses I'm used to: the ones
that comfort, fortify – even the ones that scare.

What should I be wearing? Where are my shoes?
Snowflakes like unswept rice touch my feet.
Virginal-white mountains – could be Narnia,
even Hunza Valley – raise their peaks like hands
joined together to welcome me. *Namaste*.
I can't turn back now, the storm will know.

Felice Beato Photographs the Indian Mutiny

Ashok Bery

'From the earliest days of the calotype, the curious tripod, with its mysterious chamber and mouth of brass, taught the natives of this country that their conquerors were the inventors of other instruments besides the formidable guns of their artillery, which, though as suspicious perhaps in appearance, attained their object with less noise and smoke.'

— Samuel Bourne, 'Photography in the East', 1863

Two bodies hang
like question marks

from a makeshift scaffold
on the outskirts of Lucknow.

The posts and crossbeam
frame them

on a canvas of sepia sky;
their hands are tied

behind their backs,
their heads bowed (so the pose

suggests) in the shame of those
who have not been true to their salt.

And those turbaned Sikhs looking on,
heads held high,

swords sloped
against their shoulders

as if presenting arms –
what do their poses say?

Reverence in the face of death?
The relief of the survivor?

The pride of the soldier
who has remained true to his salt?

The man with the answers
is out of the picture –

moments before,
he'd scrambled up on the gallows

to still the death throes
that were spoiling his shot.

And now it's picture perfect:
ten solemn spectators;

the frame
of posts and crossbeam;

two tranquil bodies
and a sepia sky

above a patch of scruffy ground
on the fringes of Lucknow.

The ubiquitous
photographer

is nowhere to be seen.

Felice Beato (1832–1909): British-Italian photographer who worked
mainly in Asia, including India during the aftermath of the Uprising
of 1857–58.

First Flush Darjeeling

Ansuya

Plucked by the hands of women, in turquoise,
jade and magenta saris tucked high

as they step through lush valleys of West Bengal.
Their baskets fill with leaves and buds.

I pick up a china cup between my thumb
and forefinger, inhale cinnamon, rose and ripe apple.

It's an occasion, tea from six thousand feet,
earthed in loamy soil, now curled greenish leaves

bathe in my teapot, overlooking the grey
of west London. I spoon a little honey to sweeten.

I lean back into plump cushions to savour
the smooth, elegant syrupy tea like a connoisseur.

The leaves at the bottom of the pot the shape
of India. I close my eyes and see the hands

of the women that pluck each leaf like breath
from the earth.

Ghazal: Language of Loss

Shasta Hanif Ali

I swam across oceans blue, searching for poets penning couplets on you.
   A swelling of loss.
But this language of grief, this zabaan of ghum, was not the answer to
   my loss.

Is dunya mai, yai dukh, milta hai har roz
yai ghum, mahman jaisay ata hai har roz: what is the translation of this loss?

In this world, this pain meets us every day.
This sorrow, like a visitor, comes to us every day: this translation lost in loss.

A Ramadan past, I sat reading my Quran: out flew a bird, a prayer, a
   note written by you.
Yet this bird I could not name; the note I could not read; but the dua I
   caught in these tides of loss.

Lips follow the curvature of a language inherited. Five words for death,
   ten for loss, or more.
Whole countries in my mouth, but this heart still remains tongue tied.
   I'm so sorry for your loss.

Great Grandmother,

1947

Anannya Uberoi

Below an overhang of bougainvillea
the seamstress levels a scarf –
hot winds, shilly-shallying canopy.
A thread ties her body to the ochre house.
A scarecrow draped in her tattered saree
watches on. Her day drunk husband
naps on a rope-webbed bedstead,
his quilt sewn to its most crooked patch.
Wafts of guava and Indian plum
cartwheel down the oil-lamped tracks
to the end of this makeshift world,
where a dun pony meanders.
The village owl
whistles, corncrakes gawk
at the shorn cornfield where small animals
burrow their heads
and the nerveless sun dips her pale feet
in the earth-warm pond.
The seamstress gathers up
a last stretch of linen, the ruffles of which

fluff up the farm, the hillocks,
even the burn hole moon, and rumple
the almond clouds

every so often a beribboned wagtail
pulls at a thread
that sets her floating across the sky

Half Shapes of Me

Anita Nahal

They say some families can be misfits. Like hard-boiled eggs. What to savour, what to throw. Like frost bite in warm weather. Or a nasty cold in summers. Like time differences across oceans never merging. Like mighty waves without winds surging. Like forty-eight hours mushed into twenty-four. Like the messy, friendly neighbourhood grocery store. Like ageing without learning lessons. Like a fire glowing without passions. What can I say… some things are best left alone or hidden. Like secrets in paintings and words, here and there in tit-bits. Families can be misfits.

And so, I merrily go along my days. Manufacturing sprightly yet unfulfilled poses. Like fragrance-devoid roses. Hiding self-doubts that you implanted quite early in childhood. Like concealing my side face, a hand under my chin, always. 'Your profile is so ugly,' you'd berate at home and on the school bus. All that fuss to make yourself feel fancy in your personal glitz. Your ground you stood, and I had no energy left to brood. My distress and resolve became even more real. Like a hot seal. On documents past. Like a body laying still, surreal, at a repast. Families can be misfits.

I paint half shapes of me in mismatching colours, in all the spaces and places wherever I go, leaving my DNA in rooms, emotions, and in your calls, which I dutifully pick up. Maybe you need something, I think. In the video, you don't blink, taking not a moment to complain and shame my lack of desire to visit India. I chirpily change Amrita Sher Gil's sentence and shout, 'The world belongs to me, not only India.' Families can be misfits.

Note: This poem is inspired by a sentence that Amrita Sher-Gil, a Hungarian-Indian painter is believed to have written to her friend shortly after her trip to Europe in 1934. She said, 'I can only paint in India. Europe belongs to Picasso, Matisse, Braque… India belongs only to me.' The reasons, meanings or aftermaths of the above statement is not being discussed here.

https://www.dailyartmagazine.com/amrita-sher-gil-indias-frida-kahlo/

Home is the Third Space

Hana Ormara

The First Space: Paradise
Golbag[1]

My home is paradise,
        a garden of roses set with lapis skies;
        a far-reaching sun turns our soil into gold.
        It's a place where trees grow diamonds
                and deserts flow
                with camel's milk and date syrup.

Its windows are people
        born with hardship in their blood;
        they live with generosity, undying hospitality,
                speaking an **a**ncient **l**anguage
                bursting with vitality,
                        in **p**o**etic** word.

My **h**ome **is** paradise;
        its gates **s**hield doorways to the legacy of **t**ribes.

---

1 *Golbag*: 'Eden' in Balochi.

Legendary winds have carved
our ballads into stone.

Here is a time machine
with portals to history,
and here lies the fertility
of a vast
motherland.

The Second Space: Paradise of the Invisible Ceirein[2]

My home is a chartered land,
cut by compasses
held in Empire's hands,

made a bordered paradise

subjecting life to withstand.

Where invisible children and invisible people have shattered hearts and cancelled sighs. Our invisible lives, sound unheard cries, our unknown words and endangered language are unseen footsteps on invisible maps.

My home is an invisible state.

2 *Ceirein*: 'Invisible' in Balochi.

Home is the Third Space: Being
Ast[3]
A Generation's Flight

The fright and flight from home makes sanctuary a home.
    In redbrick flower façade, we shaped a life and stayed.
When safe skies sometimes cascade with words like
    'Nasty', 'Refugee', 'Go back to where we can't see',
        there's still beauty in democracy;
'Are you talking to me? We share commonality
beyond boundaries or nationality –
        I am human, just like you.'

Custodians of a New Generation

Our home is a nomadic abode,
    our body a shell where imagination dwells.
    In our skin lives the sense of concrete permanence.

    In the absence of a home, we made family a home
                where roof adored floors,
        cherished ceilings and doors,
    with names only we understood
    in our language of home, were people of home
in memories that we owned was a self that we'd known.

---

3 *Ast*: 'Being' in Balochi.

My Being is the Third Space

My home is an unclear place –
        a vision of love, the plight of people displaced.
I have never touched the soil of my home,
        yet I have always roamed the sweet streets of my home.
I have never drunk the taste of my home,
        yet I have always breathed the air of my home.
                My home is a paradise,
                        my home is inside of me,
                        my home lives
                        in this poem.

Home

(A poem to be read aloud in a room full of racists.)

Mev Akram

Where are you from? No, I mean where are you really from?

Questions with sharp edges.

Words dipped in vinegar, resting on cuts that have not yet healed from the last time.

This IS home. She is here.

But know this too.

She has homes across oceans. And homes in the hearts of the men that have loved her.

She has even bigger homes in the minds of the men that have hated her.

The ones with the questions.

She's in there. Squatting. Rent free.

Dressed in Doc Martens and a pair of jhumke. Red lips, a nose ring, and hennaed hands.

Thick dark curls framing an earthy brown face.

Her father's nose and her mother's tongue; in more ways than one.

She laughs in urdu, prays for sabr in Arabic, then puts you in your place in YOUR tongue.

She's from the land of the Indus, the Himalayas and the Karakoram.

Of kings and queens and songs and stories of beauty and terror.

Now, home is in a city and a land that her ancestors could not have imagined.

Skies stretch out across time and space to meet the mountains that her mother's mother's mother knew.

A choice, a choice and another choice.

A thread binding continents, a hundred thousand voices echoing through history.

She walks a tightrope between there and here, then and now.

Her home is a feeling. A knowing.

Her home is vast, echoing, a chasm of emotion.

Her home is a light in her chest, glowing and growing and bursting out.

Ask her again.

Homing

Devjani Bodepudi

He told me there was no word for goodbye. Instead, we say
āsh/i:/ A promise to return. It was with the rise and fall of
the first open-mouthed vowel, an *Ah* of resignation, he knew
he had to leave.

Sh, they quieted the child, as they crossed the border at night
with the long /i:/ at the end of his own country tucked into
his shirt pocket.

They waded far away from the mustard fields they knew,
swapping them for the yellow rape that draped their new
end. Now he exclaimed *Ah* again, but in recognition, and
sang of home often, weaving the sky with paper kite tails and
mango stains that gave away his thieving. The songs would
unfurl and gather and crease around his eyes and mouth
until one day, suddenly, they stopped.

While our silhouettes hardened against the sun in our last
days as children
he exchanged his own cyanotype image for gilded versions
of me.

He had fattened me on belief.

I belonged while he fitted edgewise.

Lying on his hospital bed like withered ivy, he whispered into the cracks of living's cacophony.

Sh, he said, *there's no need to cry; losing means leaving and leaving is the promise to return.*

Sh, he said again, his now soft, cold fingers around my own. *Listen to the way we say hope.*

See? Borrowing a pen from a nurse, he wrote on a napkin.

Ā sh ā

Āshā holds a different ending entirely.

The final *ah* is everything.
That *ah* is the finally arriving.

How to Answer

Inappropriate Questions

Suchita Parikh-Mundul

1. On not having children
    a. The summer breeze is like a mother's embrace.
    b. The sun speaks in long days and warm nights.
    c. I lie in bed until I'm ready to begin.

2. On infertility
    a. Most evenings, my path is strewn with jasmine.
    b. At high tide, the sea is pregnant with waves.
    c. The sky has lost count of the stars she's birthed.

3. On whether your partner is impotent
    a. Laughter sounds like the twinkling of stars.
    b. We walk in the rain when there's nowhere to go.
    c. The wind coaxes us to waltz.

4. On your biological clock
    a. The moon's silver gaze always finds me.
    b. If I'm quiet, I can hear dewdrops.
    c. Dawn breaks like birdsong.

5. On old age
   a. Even months later, I feel the sand's undulation on my skin.
   b. The frangipani holds my childhood close.
   c. Autumn leaves can fly.

6. On legacy
   a. We grow gardens everywhere we go.
   b. Butterfly wings refract light.
   c. Breath is like the beauty of wildflowers.

India's on the Moon

Ankita Saxena

Save yourself from
the moon:
take blessings from
mah, chant *Om Som
Somaaye Namah*, offer
milk to Shiva –
take a bath
in Ganga,
dust to dust

the world's end:
honey light, titanium
God – who else could
survive a crash, beat
the atmosphere
on the darkest night,
the sky is blazing
this is what it's come to:
your mother, all craters

escape to
a side with potholes
compete with
the Russians,
in a saucer of
shadow,
blow conch shells
ashes to ashes,
all craters, your moon.

Just Before It Burns

Anita Goveas

I am alone again in the kitchen with the weight of the women who cooked this before me, who recognised the aromatic scent of spices before they burnt, when to stir and when to step away, who made this same recipe but understood that every time it was never the same, who felt joy and pain and worry and shame and lust and love and anger and fear and knew to stamp all that down inside so that the generations waiting to be fed, always waiting, always hungry, always expecting, would taste the love and nothing else.

Longevity of a Superstition

Kinshuk Gupta

Dusk. Sitting in a dented Alto, we watch birds
blacken the sky, their throats multiple metronomes.
Gusts of wind cane wheat stalks.
Smoke from Panipat refinery spreads
like a devil's silhouette in the sky. Rest – a child's
line drawing. The driver tells us about bowed workers,
from pockmarked villages where the State is liberating
statues of Birsa Munda. Clustered like buffaloes
in an afternoon pond, they wear checkered lungis,
work in farms for six months for two bags
of rice. He laughs – they drink rice water thinking milk
is a calf's share. He halts when a black cat crosses
the road. He reverses the car and folds his hands
to whichever god is not sleeping at this odd hour.
Again the emerald-eyed cat dissects our path,
casting its oblong shadow. Determined this time,
he darts the car in the cat's direction.
Trembling shrieks, chocolate-fudge blood –
the black-hole town unbothered. Let me confess,
we stare at the driver in the rear-view mirror.

And we y-a-w-n, replaying the scene in our head
when that stray cat worked its teeth on our canary
like a toddler picking at his scab. 'What you do
comes back,' we chant and ask him to hurry.

Man on the Northern Line

Naila Ali

I instinctively do up another button on my shirt as that Asian man sits down opposite me on the tube. I haven't yet seen him completely but know he is Asian. Past experience means I am on guard, mentally covering myself to become invisible so that he cannot appropriate or revel in any part of me – I belong to me and it has taken an arduous journey to reclaim all of me, for me and for those I choose to share with, but mostly for me.

I see his shoes: clean, black, Clarks maybe; I think I bought similar school shoes for my son, years ago. I remain wary as the most respectable-looking men in my community have trespassed on my mental, emotional and physical property. A pair of sensible shoes does not placate me.

My gaze continues upward upon the blue, bobbled, not wool trousers, clean and pressed but old. Old and worn. A slight softening within. Why do aged trousers invoke empathy within me? It is the limbs they cover – slight, perhaps also aged, taking so very little space not only within the cloth but also on the modest seat of the Northern Line.

The hands, always the hands. The carriers of our stories in each finger, each ageing line, each growing liver spot, each bulging vein increasing in size as the skin gets thinner and elasticity becomes a friend we once knew. The hands signalled hard work and weariness, the digits no longer able to straighten fully giving a wizard-like quality to his appendages. The crêpey skin enveloping his story. If a loved one cradled his hand against their cheek, closed their eyes and listened, would they hear his story? If his rasping fingers stroked their head, as is the tradition in our communities, would they inherit the history?

I looked up, straight ahead, I looked at all of him. There it was – his complete story conveyed in a single, photographic frame. A man child. He appeared not to have grown since puberty. Adult clothes in a child's size. A shirt that was not too shabby at all, perfectly pressed, completing a uniform that men in my family and community seemed reluctant to give up. Stay press trousers, smart shirt, work shoes. But they never worked in offices, not here, not back home. How, why did the second and further generations retain that uniform, the rebellions of the teens and twenties reverting back to 'dad' clothes?

Where did his story begin? At the top? His jet-black dyed hair cohabiting with the inch-long white roots, a futile attempt to hold on to youth. The lack of volume, fullness, shine and vibrancy a reminder of things that cannot be controlled.

His thin, slight, gaunt and lined face uneasily fidgeting with a face mask, putting it on, pulling it down and then back up, losing one side, feeding it back around his ear. It gave me a glimpse of a thin, black perfectly groomed black (dyed?) moustache that reminded me of my father. He did this dance all the while holding a piece of paper in his other hand, which remained suspended, frozen in space while he and the train moved around it. I wondered what it was. Directions, instructions, a letter? I hoped it was a letter of joy and love, but his demeanour suggested otherwise. He gazed at it, perhaps he wasn't reading at all, placed it in his lap and put his un-stretched, outstretched right hand over his heart. Did he mean to do that? There was not much weight to the gesture – his elbow did not anchor on his lap or stomach, his hand did not quite rest on his breast. He raised his left hand around his neck, as though he was going to hold it, but the fingers did not unravel so he just placed it alongside. I noticed some tape on his thumb. Had he ever been embraced, had he ever embraced another, could he even bear it?

That is how I left that Asian man, the one lost in his reverie, the one who didn't look at me, for which I was grateful. I mused where his journey began, what he had witnessed, where he was as he sat lost on that tiny, Northern Line seat.

Missing

Clare Ramsaran

In black-and-white photographs
from 1950s Maida Vale, he faced his future,
in light-coloured slacks and a clean white shirt,
not yet indentured to an immigrant's job –
in the days when his stay in this country
was only for a short time.

Years later, in our family home
I stand by the bathroom door,
watching my father shave –
a last leisurely male bastion
in this feminised household.

His brush swishes around the bowl
which holds foam, the colour of icing sugar,
the colour of egg whites.

He gently paints spiralling circles on his face,
one finger in the cleft of his chin,
tipping his head up.
His eyes contemplate the ceiling
while he pulls his razor in scratching upstrokes,
skimming a taut Adam's apple.

The razor clinks against the sides of a chipped china mug
as he swirls the excess foam away.

Lifting the razor to his face once more
he unearths another swathe
of smooth brown skin
from the layer of white.

Later – alone –
my fingertips reach for
the salt-and-pepper bristles
of his shaving brush,
dry at night,
damp by day.

Over the years, there were times of plenty –
of collar-tickling waves of black hair,
those curls that could not be tamed –
my legacy.

He sported luxuriant sideburns
and a bandit's moustache.
The sideburns came and went –
like flares and space hoppers and the Bay City Rollers.
But the moustache stayed.

Once, however,
he emerged from his morning ritual
with something not quite right.
His unseen upper lip,
newborn naked and exposed,
remnants of the missing moustache
clinging to his razor,
gurgling down our protesting drains.

Mother/Tongue

Madri Kalugala

my mother tells everyone that I called a document for a land
deed, in Sinhala, a 'භූමි කම්පාව'.[1] I didn't. She brings this
up in random conversations with faceless people who I barely
know, and laughs: her trilling social laugh of floaty powder
puffs and heady perfume – and yet again this becomes a
'story' that defines me, narrated by others, that will go down
in history. As always, she thinks it's funny, it's cute – posh,
maybe – the little girl who 'can't speak Sinhala', 'grew up
abroad, you know', 'සිංහල හරියට බෑ'[2] – but the English!
Phew, her English, ah... 'කිට්ටු කරන්නවත් බෑ.[3]
අම්මත් ඉතින් English teacher නේ.'[4]

---

1 භූමි කම්පාව: 'Bhuumi kampaawa': 'Earthquake' (Sinhala). The
correct word, in the context of this conversation, should be 'Bim Saviya':
which refers to a legal document, a title deed of land in Sri Lanka.

2 සිංහල හරියට බෑ: 'Sinhala hariyata baa': 'Can't speak Sinhala
properly.'

3 කිට්ටු කරන්නවත් බෑ: 'Kittu karannawath baa': 'No one can come close
to/match her English.' (Usually said with admiration.)

4 අම්මත් ඉතින් English teacher නේ: 'Mother is also an English teacher,
you know!'

I am thirty-three.

I know what I did and didn't say. The words still come to me
hesitatingly, yes, and I have to first hold them in the open jar
of my mouth and taste them like sour olives, roll
them on my tongue and feel their texture and shape –
maybe even bite into them sometimes
and test the feel – before I spit

them out – but I am old enough to know the difference
between an earthquake and a title deed. My body becomes
a fist and clenches tightly: I say, I did not say that, but the
conversation has already become a ship and sailed off into
open waters without me. So the lid screws itself closed on
the mouth of the jar full to bursting, and my mouth becomes
a deep-belly cave full of echoes of all the words I want to
speak/ the sentences forming inside my head/
the languages warring like ancient gods inside my brain/
to express all the things no one will listen to me say,

like: I did not choose this. Like: I love my mother

tongue and its words move me in a belly-aching way that
English somehow cannot
touch – but it was lost to me. Lost to me, my beautiful
Sinhala tongue: it slips through my fingers like a wet
eel that I keen to grasp
and be

electrocuted by –

big blue bolts of electricity, that I wade through slimy waters
knee-deep looking for it with my hands dunked in seaweed,
that I swim, leagues underwater – chasing that

fluorescent light –

in the hopes that I might

catch it

and feel that surge of split-white current through me.

Like: when I was taken from my country and my damp
roots sunk by forceful fingers into another land, I had no
tongue to form the words. No language to call my own,
and no one who understood me; strange brown girl with
dusky skin and wood-apple eyes, and a heart that reeked
of fish and wet sand and saltwater. Like: how they told me
I should be proud to speak the English tongue – but I did
not, then, understand: why did the saltwater rise in my
brown-child's eyes when I heard the songs of a country
they said I'd left behind?

Like: being robbed of my language made me, mother,

so *godforsakenly lonely* –

I don't say this because it's in fashion.

Oh, I say this because the language sings in me, has always
sung to me: my slippery newborn Sinhala that was stolen
away from me, still raw and bathed in my wet dark blood.

And because cracks have appeared in the jar:
the sour olives have fermented in the brine, bitter-green
and acrid, and are this –

this – close to bursting.

Muṣallā[1]

In Memory of Nawab Asaf-ud-Daula

Abhijeet

Half-Lakhori,[2]
Half-a Nawab's flesh. His prayers
Measure the minarets back and forth,
Asking gods to release him from longing.
He saunters in its stained corridors.

Pigeons circle the mosque,
Children race to and fro, without knowing they touch
Nawab's feet and come back to his memory. Here
In the lawns of Imam-bargah. Under the henna
Of falling autumn leaves. Courtesans are crying.

Laid on the very lawns, with their peace, are
Elderly djinns, snoring years with every breath. Every sigh.
Lovers visit them for blessings. Between them
Faith lives. Nobody has seen it, the faith.
Although love can be spotted, which is always a relief.

---

1 *Muṣallā*: A prayer-mat; a place to pray.

2 *Lakhori*: A kind of clay brick from Indian subcontinent; used predominantly in Mughal architecture.

Every now and then, sky opens and washes the dome.
Rain falls in the courtyard, like a dancer.
People run to the shades near the passages of Baoli;
Lovers flourish the dance. Children are asked to look elsewhere.
Pigeons bathe. The decrepit Lakhori drinks her death.

Tourists leave. Pilgrims bow and walk out. Children
Disappear with crowd. Women have departed in their
Shrouds. Djinns have turned their backs to the architecture.
Isha[3] calls them. Mosque feels nothing. Half-a Nawab's flesh does.
His prayers have kept the structure from collapsing.

---

3 *Isha*: The last and fifth of the five Islamic prayers.

my parents come from a place that

no longer exists

Rishika Williams

my parents come from a place that no longer exists

and in the 'o' of exodus I hear my father as a boy
'just take your hands,' I hear him say

and I had not heard that he had said that before
but I know him so well he does still tell me things

things that had no language before, as his memories
get younger, the further Dad goes, he ages closer

my Dad is always closer than ever before and my families
left Sind as the British penned a long line of a couplet

their lawyer came to strip off our linens to unmake our beds
to make us leave without a pot or a pen, to turn our backs

on Lali Bhai's garden, leave the books we were given, our shops
and our businesses, as they gave away our river, the very one

that named our land: aj raat the navy separates, the fabric rips
I spill some of my indigo as that part of India went

am I supposed to feel better, Cyril
that you said 'I nearly gave you Lahore'

the largest mass migration of human beings as animals
scrambling to cross a line for survival, over the amputated

shoulder of Mother India, her pallu cross-stitched wet red
as her border derailed millions in massacres of threads

un-woven warp of the Indus with the stench of departure still
lingering as Yardley's English Lavender in torn cashmere

is rape not enough: bullets still land in cargo trains
my five-year old mother sleeps clutching a biscuit tin

gold coins are inedible, the new scars indelible
invisible ink of my genes smudged in the parting

Sindoor in a hair line is to consecrate a wedding, to live in sin
is to live together as if married, yet Sind has been ashed

in vermillion, dakoon at Marwar Junction bang on the carriages
my Uma starts bleeding; she must change trains to a hospital

fugitive paints run in ajrak, must they or must they not be
rescinded, my twelve-year-old father has been left to fend for

himself; he cuts logs for a torn piece of bread, to break with his
siblings; an unbroken promise kept to his mother, right up to no end

Dad,

I don't understand what I'm writing: how can I hear the
sitars' lyrics caterwauling, the tabla beats reverberating as
history migrates our tanpura I hear now as violins, as I tiptoe
amongst the neem, golden shower, pipal and moringa trees,
honestly, what is this strange tense that we find ourselves in

I sit with you to listen to the ghazals of Anup Jalota
I watch you in the garden, I see you talking with Dada
I deal us a hand of rummy, time to play cards with Uma
I reach for a mango near the rose bush, I choose you a flower
I will feed you your breakfast, yes
I know you'd like some seyun patata
I hold your hands Dad and rewhisper

'we are all safe as we re-member'

Power

Nikita Aashi Chadha

content warning: use of racial slur

never knowing where to place my body. when to allow
my real self to appear. switching between codes and roles
because anything is better than being myself. learning too
young that myself isn't enough. it's never felt like it's enough.
dreams of finding a space where i finally feel free. where my
existence isn't a mantle that hangs around my neck. feeling
out of place in all of my homes. the houses where my family
live and dwell. the kingdom i was born in that will never
see me as a citizen because my skin is glorious and brown
and not pale and stale. the country that my people come
from that still feels alien to me when i visit. they call me *gori*
back home which stings much more than *paki* ever did. at
least when i was younger i could tell people that their racism
was inaccurate. this was before discovering the lines drawn
clumsily across my country that separate us from each other
and ourselves. learning about partition made me feel more
connected than i ever have, which is ironic considering how
little i know about how it impacted my family or how they
felt at the time. i know my Nanis were both born in Lahore,
which no longer exists because of colonial maps and stuffy

white men with stiff upper lips who decided that this space was theirs for the taking. like a mango beaten and pulped to be eaten through pursed lips; this is how these men thirst for my country and all of its beauty. they want to control it and they want to control me, but how can you control wildfire? how can you tame something that will destroy you and everything in its path and leave behind your legacy of nothing? that's what you deserve and what you will have when the dust settles and modern history runs its course. it will be you that bounces around homeless. stateless. it will be your languages and customs that will be consumed. eradicated. your traditional clothes will become costumes that my grandchildren will wear as they run around with exaggerated british accents. the sadness as i realise that my hybridity and seizing of two worlds has left me more colourless than i was before. the amount of rituals, histories that i won't pass down to my children because i just don't know them. a tongue that cannot grasp consonants because i was never taught how. wanting to try but fighting my own shame at not knowing. being shamed by countless cornershop uncles that claim it's for my own good but i know what it's about. it's about power.

it's always about power.

Romanticising My life as I Hang the Washing Out to Dry

In memory of Valsamma Unni 1951–2024

Jay Mitra

I hear the chickens before I see them.
The squawking and clucking pierces
a symphony of flute-like tweeting –
a battle of birdsong and then

white plumage sails through the green.
Small chubby bodies are a feathery boat
mid-rock, as if a wave had carried the mast
of their neck upwards and then frozen,

turned invisible. My grandma lives in the jungle,
and sometimes I am scared to look up,
to take in the cracks of her ceiling,
the spiders that cling to the corners

like frayed rope. Last night we awoke
to a crash of coconuts on the roof above her bed.
My brother and mum burst into the living room
where grandma slept. She was fine –

no hole in the wooden sky, no mass
of cracked husk and flesh on her sheets.
Later that day, as I hang out the washing to dry,
I romanticise my life. I think of my grandma

taking my mum's hand to subdue her fear,
how, in hushed Malayalam, she whispered
confidently: *I pray every night.*
Don't worry. God will protect me.

Round 25

Humus

I was a black belt at fifteen –
The highest of the colour grades,
It holds strength, power, versatility;
A colour we respect,
But does not reflect
In what we see.
But no one told me
That my first spar
Would be with society,
That infected my parents minds
To believe
The melanated was not good enough for me.

Opening up to your parents is a blessing –
Letting them into your life
So you don't have to lie –
But that's something I'm regretting…

They said,
'Do as you please after I'm dead
Or leave and forget our relationship now.
If you want your happiness

You're not my daughter,
You're a disgrace to the family.
This Black person you're with
Is bound to be…
Unsuccessful, uneducated and unreliable.
It's just not the done thing for any family of mine.
I told you, I don't want black blood in my blood line.'

Disowned, exposed,
Struggling to regrow
From the deep guilt I was thrown
Into.
Welcome to the Asian confessional,
Where being honest
Makes you realise love is conditional.

With this constant heartache
Was a man who refused to let me break,
Smiled through all the racist sh*t.
I know it was hard –
Harder than he'd admit.
He prioritised me, held me, fed me
On the days I couldn't eat;
He knew being disowned
Came with feeling incomplete.

I'm telling you,
He really was my Man-ifestation,
Cos there's really no explanation
For that type of love vibration,
Full of love, care, support and appreciation.

So I'll never overstand why their hate and rejection
Is never met with any self-reflection,
To prioritise my happiness
Over his melanated complexion.

I'd get it if he's rude, a bum or not good for my health and soul,
But they didn't even know his name
Before they reversed their parental roles.
They stay uninvolved,
Because I chose love over family –
I mean, love over racism and irrationality.

I did everything to make them proud:
Graduated, licence, a job;
Who knew this one choice of mine
Would run that all into the ground.
My achievements, my only-child status no longer matters;
They can't find the strength within,
Even if he had the purest heart,
The martial to my art,
It can't change the sin on his skin –
That's all they see.

People of today would say I'm breaking generational curses,
Breaking the cycle.
I know it sounds cool,
But don't be fooled –
It's a fight for survival.
A fight no one really prepared me for:
To fight against people I absolutely adore,
With every outcome feeling like I've tapped out on the floor.

It's normal to be afraid cos it's a lonely ride;
Have faith and belief you're doing what's right.
Sometimes you are your own opponent –
You versus you –
To fight against giving in to those with a different view.
Sometimes it gets too much,
To meet standards and fight the suppression;
Sometimes you lose touch and forget
You are nobody's possession.
So fight for your beliefs
And create your own storyline;
Soon that bell will ring
And it's a win for you this time.

Shiva Explains to Parvati Why Their Son Looks Different

Vijaya Venkatesan

Look, I said I'm sorry, babes; what else can I say? I've said it
till I'm blue in the face. If you flippin' let me get a word in.
I'd just come into the inner courtyard, OK, and this
mouthy kid, I didn't recognise him, right, right, that's on me.
But be fair, I've been away a couple of years,
and I tell you, after the high mountain air the plains' heat
fried my brain. It's no excuse, but I've just stepped inside
from that furnace in the street, and I'm home and into shade,
like chilled beer, it felt, and this kid starts with the Who are you,
my mother is having her oil bath and she's left me in charge,
and you can't just barge in here and anyway, who are you?
And I lost it, I put my hands up to it, I lost it. I opened
my third eye just for a sec and there he was, a pile of ashes,
and then I saw your jewellery all piled up in a heap
behind where he'd been standing, and it hit me
who his mother was and – babes, don't look at me
like that, it all happened so quickly.

I put it right, didn't I. He's standing before us, isn't he. Yes,
he now has an elephant's head, but I asked all creatures
and the only one who was willing to give its life was that
elephant. I gathered clumps of the turmeric-stained
besan you'd used to scrub the oil from your skin before
you went into the bathhouse. I picked it all up so carefully,
every scrap, moulded his little body, but it wasn't enough,
there wasn't enough, and so I went out into that blasted heat
and begged everyone I came across for a head for our son.

I've sorted it with our boy. He'll have a shrine in the forecourt
of every one of my temples, and he'll be the main muse and scribe
for all poets — he's cool with that. And you know kids, they get used
to some pretty strange things really quickly. So, we're good?

Spring in Copenhagen

Rishi Dastidar

Ecstatic we sail on the sea of blossom
Selfies under trees, proof we once blossomed

Under the gaze of the bored and entranced
The fairy tale of waiting for your princess blossoms

Laurel wreaths by statues, faded to forgotten brown
We struggle to remember our finest blossom

Drawn to unassuming churches that hide their gilt
Until you are pew-side, to ask for awe and blossom

With open arms I switch on schlarach low frequency
By a blue coffee stand where the Irma girl blossoms

I am annihilating time and space again
In the hope that somewhere else I will blossom

Tea

Koushik Banerjea

Your eyes would light up every day at this time
Loose leaves no slang
Sublime infusion from Darjeeling sprang
Better health, less wobble, nothing too much trouble
Your heart so much bigger than that open door, its liggers

Khali haat no matter, pure habit not butter
Kemon accho, bhai, do sit down
Stop fussing, take a plate, put away that frown
Have some tea and a sandesh
The windows? Pay no mind, just some wire mesh
Mostly youngsters, not all like that
Badmaash families, but you know what's what
No? Surprised, but happy for you
That taste's as homegrown as the soil from which it grew

Oh this? It's Darjeeling, old country with feeling
Really? Thik, I'll pop the kettle back on
Samosa while you're waiting, memory taste drawn
Tetley, two sugars, bag left in to brew
Only so long, it's cha, bhai, not casserole, nor stew

My home your wishes, oh, that's my eldest doing the dishes
The younger one's over there now
Likes his tea, also likes a row
Helped his dad with the wire mesh then went out to play
His mind's steady, it's mine that started to fray
Drank my tea, heard my own brother
'Garam cha, Didi, you're their ma, but try not to smother'
Just boys, they need to do that
Not locked up, in this flat

Prayer beads every time
They killed that boy in Southall – don't want it to be one of mine
Why worry cha on tastebuds, but worry I always do
Bricks kissing windows, through the letterbox something undue
Eldest keeps an eye out but his brother can be wild
Few limits to his fury – no longer a little child

He's a boy who's seen plenty over whom I've little sway
Out there doing something, maybe guilty soon of affray?
Drinks tea like a grown-up, though he's barely even a teen
Keeps stressing what's blown up – only God knows what he means

Teatime means no tea here, illogic its main dish
A different world, harder, long before newscasters called Krish
Fancy word, illogic? I know, found it while using Dettol
Sickness sad nostalgia on my tongue, a little menthol
Loved the taste of it, the look of it, made me feel so alive
Purity its own horror against which to always strive
Impure thoughts, unclean rug, our presence here not exactly snug

Yet I scrubbed away the evidence; no one would ever know
Daily disinfectant, across the threadbare a throw
Dried eyes over tea, strong, sugary broth
Wanted no one to see me, past façade to the wrath

This stranger in my home now, and he's already backing away
Mere mention of my youngest, about whom I've more to say
Talk to him – he doesn't bite, just the heat in the equation
Tea and a slice, cut lip, on a good day no abrasion
Some kind words, or interest, anything but a slight
One thing though, bhai, be forewarned, likes his tea just right

You're gone now and I'm still here
Can't lie, Ma, there were some tears
You'd have laughed, though
All these faces from the past
Round your home
Drinking tea, not built to last
Of Himalayas, the foothills barely a trace
Just bags brewed like tar
And I know you're back with the good stuff now, however far
No more worries, no more fright
A perfect brew, Ma
Just right

The Face in Flight

Sav Altair Hamid

The mirror is a well I lower myself into each evening, turning my face in my hands like something between a sculptor and a lover. Both are waiting for the object of their caress to bloom with revelation. My face catches the fullness of the day's dying light lingering like a lipstick stain beyond my window. I have my mother's mouth and my father's brow and eyes I thought were my own until I bore witness to their reflection in yours and I realised they belonged to you all along. Under sundown lustre the face takes flight – Dorian reversed. No stubble pricks my fingers; planted seeds sprout soft shadow across my jaw. Bone chisels angle from baby fat. The clay is pliable between my palms, shifting weight from cheek to neck as sunrays sizzle concrete. I feel as the first. I have never seen the fledging in a skin like mine. Never felt what they called euphoria until I saw myself in my first sharp-collared black kameez and I understood it is just another word for homecoming. I stand like nobody but myself. At once sculptor and sculpted, lover and the desired.

The Hat

Mediah Ahmed

My father's father's hat. 'Jinnah's hat.' Proper name: Karakul[1] hat.
Lies still in the cupboard.
(Only to be taken out for special occasions.)
This is the hat of great religious figures and politicians.
Passed down from generation to generation, gathering the sweat
    of past ancestors.
The hat is made of black wool, with a shiny cream silk lining with
    gold stitching, fit for a king.
A black crown.
A hat which still smells of perfume, reminding me of mehfils and
    jalsas.
The smell which invokes fearlessness, as revolutionary na'arey are
    chanted against the British.
The label is so faded, no one can trace back who wore the hat
    first.
A representation of my lineage.
A hat cherished and well looked after.
My dad wore this hat when he was a child; even though it was
    oversized and fell over his face, he was his dad.

---

1 *Karakul*: Written also as Qaraqul.

My father's hat. 'Trilby hat.' Also known as a fedora.

Lies still in the cupboard.

(Only to be taken out for special occasions.)

This is the hat of jazz, blues, soul musicians and Indiana Jones.

Passed down from generation to generation, gathering the sweat
of past ancestors – brought from a second-hand shop.

The hat is made of brown rabbit-hair felt, with a shiny dark
brown silk lining, bound with a black ribbon.

A brown crown.

A hat which still smells of perfume, reminding me of Eid prayers
and funerals.

The smell which invites angels, as they also pray with you.

A representation of a new culture or a fusion of East and West?

A hat cherished and well looked after.

I wore this hat as a child; even though it was oversized and fell
over my face, I was my dad.

My hat. 'Straw hat.' Also known as a bonnet.

Lies still in the cupboard.

(Taken out for any occasion.)

This is the hat perfect for summer and latest fashion (in those
days).

I'm the first in my generation to wear this hat.

The hat is made of reeds, bound with a yellow ribbon.

A golden crown.

A hat reminding me of discos, birthdays and Christmas parties.

A representation of the next generation of youth.

A hat cherished and well used.

I wore this hat as a child – perfect fit.

The Unnamed Road

Jaspreet Mander

She talked of years gone by
the early-fifties primary school
a separate entrance for girls
how dad's was the last word on everything
mum's reservations hung limply in the air
how eggshell stares at home hardened
when she announced acting was her calling
the trepidation that set off and thudded on
as she stepped into the lane
from the repertory theatre late evening
three times a week
how the hammering above her ribcage pounded
as she stood in the packed bus
a boneless thing pushing into her rear
relentless till she got off at the stop
how the famous director religiously catered
to the male protégés' doubts and queries
hers routinely brushed off
'Inconsequential,' the acclaimed arch of his brow said
how her suggestion was duly heard and ignored
at the insurance company
the selfsame idea by a male colleague

a fortnight later
was hailed sheer brilliance
the like of which the chair had not come by in years

I told her of the seething fury
locked in my chest all these years
the storm that unleashed
when I reached home after nine in the evening
if ever the grandfather clock in the living room
struck ten or, the rare instance, eleven
and I wasn't yet home
Mum would sit with a prayer on her lips
heart in her mouth
fearing the worst, molestation, rape
family honour besmirched, latter the absolute horror
a fate worse than death
I told her how 1980s hungry ogles
seared as I donned jeans
bicycled to college
how I used to walk
not on the left but right side of the road
to make sure I saw what was coming my way
not let an ugly shock take over
and stupefy my senses
how in the dark back lane
not far from our house
I was walking, for once, on the left
and a man coming from behind
grabbed my breast
didn't let go
till I shrieked in mindless pain
and slumped on the pavement

it wasn't just rage and disgust
there rose an abhorrence clawing at my throat
looking for a phrase, a word
I couldn't find a single one
that fitted my humiliation
how the venerated academic
supervising my research assignment
called me to his flat
just as the first five pages
were read and rubbished
he took off his trousers
dunking his thumbs into his knickers

We look into each other's eyes
smoky blue and pitch black
blink away our tears
trying hard to smile
hers slow and wan
mine ghostly and fleeting
we gather our clipboards, notepads, biros
decades, years, moments
still to be spoken and shared
our ignominies still to be scraped and binned
another meet another day
we sellotape our indignities and angers
thrust them into our tote bags
velcro the top edges
nothing should sneak into oblivion

Our noses sniffing and pink
tears pushed deep into our throats
we step out

it's pouring as far as we can see
she clicks open her umbrella
ours to share
we tuck arms into each other's
loosely at first and then closer and tighter
first and third worlds in perfect sync
we veer off the thoroughfare
walking across the village green
rain smells of earth
perching on blades of grass
clear-eyed raindrops glint
as they catch slanting headlights
we negotiate a roundabout
rain descends in solid swaying sheets
the dark devours the distant lights
nibbling the tiny dots closer at hand
windows of passing cars and buses
opaque as steam scrawls motifs
that make no sense
we peer hard for signage
scouring the stretch for pointers
left and right
as our glasses mist up
we stop looking through the lenses

The unnamed road we walk on
is not well lit
it has puddles and potholes
patches strewn aplenty
resolute we press on

These Things Are Complicated

After Richard Siken's 'Real Estate'

Lavanya Arora

Divorce without societal consequences hasn't reached our part of the world yet, especially for women. So, even if she wanted, my mother couldn't have got it. Not that she would have wanted it. She wanted nothing else but to be married, have a family. She can't even fathom holding a cigarette, let alone lighting it using the kitchen stove, something I suspect she knows I have done several times but stays mum about it. She did mutter a lot under her breath. Eventually, my father died, but unlike the man in your story, he was very much my father. Then she died too, but the world doesn't know about it yet. This isn't a Bollywood drama, but there are days when she still waits for him to return, like a blank page forebodes a footnote even before the author has conceptualised the plotline.

At his wake, when the first and second rounds of sobbing were finished, a woman — the wife of my father's only childhood friend — started listing down her children's accomplishments. If I had a punch to get mean on, I would have. But they don't serve alcohol at wakes in our part of the world yet. 'These things are complicated,' said a relative with a religion-laced heart. Perhaps some sense of social obligations too. I wasn't allowed to have a death wish for another person in my heart at my own father's wake. 'These things are complicated,' said my father's childhood friend after suggesting I listen to his guru because he's all about spirituality, not religion. I had always laughed internally at his cowardice and thoughtful manipulation, but this time I let out a hearty laugh, startling the comparative accomplishments of their children. I refrained from telling him that spirituality is an offshoot of religion just like ASMR is an offshoot of hardcore porn, not because I knew he wouldn't understand the reference, but because my father was a religious person and we were at his wake. Instead, I thought about all the ways I could die unexpectedly. Follow the footsteps of my father. I wouldn't want any confusion around it. All the details would be mentioned in a letter I purposely stopped from sending out at the last minute because I realised one of my partners wouldn't like the font.

Things I Remember When I Am Alone:

Yearning for Oman

Priyanka Sacheti

I wonder if the sofa still sits outside the house at
Seeb beach, that ungainly, lumbering creature,
older than the banyan tree growing next to it.
They both loved salt – or at least, I think they did.
I never once saw the sofa and tree talk,
but they must have, exchanging stories by the dozen:
of jinns hiding in the banyan tree's uncombed hair
and all those who sought refuge in the sofa on
moonless nights to break into hard, jagged sobs,
knowing they were heard at long last.

I wonder if the bougainvillea growing
outside my old house
is still as fuchsia as ever,
the acacia tree still twisting like a
hundred year-old yogi in deep meditation.
Pregnant cats must still nap inside dusty nests of
discarded plastic roses, unborn kittens kicking
the insides of their tender tortoiseshell-white bellies.
And the undulating hills which bear graves of dead seas

and birth tiny mauve flowers: are they still there too?
Or have they long gone the way of their forebears,
reincarnated as pastless buildings smelling of varnish?

I wonder if the mannequins in the Al Khod textile shops
still dress in their Eid Best every single day of the year,
immured in their glass aquariums. Trust me:
if you smile at them, they will smile back.
The ones sheathed in white clouds of wedding tulle,
they are too petrified, though: beneath their flaking skin,
you can hear their hearts thudding in fright. At night,
when darkness sets and they are now free to weep,
they dream of fleeing to the sea and becoming fish.
Who will tell them that fish too will be eaten one day?

I wonder if the tarmac and pavements and the desert
remember the shape of my feet. I wonder if they
remember all the times I saw through them,
as if I was walking on air,
writing in the spaces between lines.
Below my feet, I still see
a squashed tomato, days-old crushed cigarette,
an escaped straw, a Chips Oman packet,
a suffocated Sun Top carton and
crumbs from a half-eaten Switz bakery cake.
I can smell the heat rising from the moon-white earth,
like a trapped bubble, waiting to exhale.

I believe I remember everything, but the more I remember,
the less I do. I think of the big tree growing in the middle
of a chalky square, its flowers smelling sweet and unreal.

I walked past it every evening, pretending its fallen flowers
were fairy umbrellas protecting me from imaginary rain.
When I was fifteen years old they cut down the tree,
but I saw it haunting that square for years.
I can still see it now.
But little did the tree or I know
that I would become a ghost too,
wondering if the streets and
the sea and the bougainvillea
would ever see me.
One day I will become paler and paler
until I turn into dust,
and there will be nothing left to say;
see, she too was once of this earth.

The truth is that even ghosts have to die one day.

This Bride

Rupinder Kaur Waraich

Is she Priti Sapru – the Panjabi actress? Can't be –
she's wearing a red lengha with golden gota patti,
not a red salwar with a fancy jacket to go with her kameez.
This woman has jasmine flowers wrapped around her bun
and a nose ring. Her eyes are cast down with coralish shadow –
was that a look back then?

All the auntiyan are coming to see her; I wish she would smile.
She'd look even more like Preeti Sapru, like in *Aasra Pyar Da*.
Her large red bindi outlined in white, with smaller versions
enunciating her eyebrows – reminds me of how girls
are wearing them on insta but with jeans and saree blouses.
I prefer a black dot bindi – it bangs with everything.

This woman's face is sweaty; Preeti Sapru never had a sweaty face.
This woman's hands unfold intricate, incantations of mehndi.
They say, the darker the stain, the more your husband will love you.

Tholaintha Porudkal

(Lost Things)

Tehnuka

1. These losses come with the life you lead

A favourite book drenched in the rain as you run for the bus,
A headtorch – your beloved simulacrum of the sun –
dropped in deep water in a far-off dark cave,
The friend whose number you still have, but don't call,
hours and years that accelerate without reprieve,
White-haired mourners outside a funeral home,
Grass and clay soil under bare young feet –

Known losses with a wholesome grief.

2. Then there's what you experience, but cannot keep:

Voice of the spinach man, vēddi¹ folded at knees
rivalling fishmongers' calls on dusty streets
Black specks of ants invading white sugar
and fresh coconut grated by your grandmother
Lemon-icing-filled biscuits
in squashy yellow packets

---

1 *vēddi*: Dhoti.

hanging from walls of ramshackle shacks
where you walk in broken sandals
to spend your uncle's rupees.
Old books with old-book smell, devoured by cousins
who compete for words with creeping rāmapānam.[2]

One day you'll lose that word too,
And where you said Rāma's arrow, only know silverfish.

3. What was lost before it was ever told

Other books are long gone, negligible war victims:
stories won in school competitions
that your ammā and her sisters loved,
read and reread with passion
and magazine serials your grandfather cut and bound
abandoned in would-be short-term retreat.
We leave differently when we might return.
(Compare, the pāddā[3] caretaking the kōyil[4] grounds

who, smiling, says, 'I crawled here
with naught but my ID card in my pocket'
because when there is nothing more to lose
we cannot hope to return).

These bindings were cut by family knives
so you can live with these losses
not be lost with other lives

---

2 *rāmapānam*: Silverfish.

3 *pāddā*: Grandfather/old man.

4 *kōyil*: Temple.

Thus in all the stories your aunts hold
are arrow-holes missing of what
was lost before it was ever told.

Like: that on your parents' wedding day
were bloody bodies and curfews
When half a lifetime later you watch the news
there are still bloody bodies but yours

is not among them. And it will
always be a secret shame that
you escaped your birthright.

4. Losses you are ashamed to bear

You escaped your birthright for a world where you can
choose to adventure in darkness because you always have light
> (but you depend on simulacra here. In bleak places
> the sun and your bones are weak).

Escapees can await old age
and mourn what's lost with dignity
> (but you also lose old stories at a funeral celebration
> where the language is foreign and the mourners, strangers).

You can let friends move on, and never call
> (but you grieve those who could have been, disappeared
> or dead in cages).

With your passport you can safely waste time
at airline check-ins, army checkpoints, police checking
– and you never have to close the hurricane lamp,
> though you have no power, to
> huddle in dark night-time fearing intrusion
> from soldiers in green uniforms

beneath whose ground-thundering guns
you have no power
(but you still have no power).

5. Escape is a loss, too

and the gods you've never believed in.
Now, their temples in forced excavation,
your anger is a different devotion.
You, here, unbelieving in Muruga – equally as in Christ, because
    also lost
    is the belief there are saviours –
    can believe these gods and their kōyil are yours.
To be yours, they needn't be believed in.

There are loftier deities – equality, justice –
who you believed and lost faith in.

6. What you gained

Yours is a different devotion; to live is not a sin
What is your loss (ants or words or cousins or gods)
is your parents' willing trade. That you be lost
in your birthplace, that your homeland be lost to you,
and though you can live, you'll always feel
the losses they knew. But to live –
to live free is miracle, not sin. Pāvam;[5]
such bargains must be made.

---

5 *Pāvam*: Poor thing/sin.

[9 2]

(To Make or Keep Separate)

Manjot Dhaliwal

I took the cards that were dealt
but didn't play
well, I'd found a trump card, hadn't I

Wining was not so straightforward
there was a split
then a reshuffle

We threw the cards back with haste
and the blindfolded execution
of stumbling in the dark

The first play
is always
a risk
tokens of heart and spade
laid out on the table

And you need
courageous thoughts
like, maybe I could play this time
and win

Anyways, maybe winning
and losing
are both
trajectory lines
meeting up and mixing

with every gain a loss

To Speak, Without the Cacophony

of Sounds

Emmett Mehaboob

In Kerala, ginger-haired Christopher makes the local news
for passable fluency
(On Instagram, he archives the etymology of every word for
brother: *chettan, aattan, icha and annan*)

In the living room, I curse my grandfather for knowing six
languages and teaching me none
(On WhatsApp, he poorly hides his pride that his children
can now afford to forget, transplant and abandon)

In London, I trip over words like *inculcate, hermeneutical* and
dialectical while I try to explain the world
(On my own, I contemplate why it's called *pursuing* a master's,
like mastery is something to conquer or chase or it slips away)

In the Vietnamese restaurant, the owner's daughter translates
her homework at the counter
(On stumbling through my order, I wonder if it's the language
of her mother or teacher that brings relief)

(On the first bite, I wonder if her versatility nourishes joy or familiarity or resentment)

(On the drunk ride home, I contemplate how straddling two worlds is a stroke of luck, curse and anomaly)

In the writing workshop, I struggle to explain how I hate Xiaolo Gu describing sex with her white lover as *consenting colonisation*
(On paper, I acknowledge that perhaps there is contempt in almost recognition, like a photograph purposefully skewed to obscure the subject)

(Which is to say: haven't I always sought to share beds with people who carry none of the baggage I do?)

(And: the one time a boy tried to learn Malayalam it cut right to the bone. All the humiliation of intimacy couldn't compare to his careful attempt of common words: ikka, monu *and* ponne)

In the kitchen, I pick up Hindi vocabulary by listening to preachers who want me dead
(On the news, reporters inform us that the right wing uses words of peace to justify littering the street with bodies: *seva, rashtra, kula dharma*)

In the dark, I am afraid maybe there is nothing left to say

(On the phone, on screen, on the news, on consideration, upon speech and in silence, I admit that I want language to behave as both identity and suture; want to wade through its rivers and take up its shape without any complicated histories and messy proximities)

(Which is to say: I want to speak without the cacophony of sound)

In the noise of my body, on the plains of native tongue,
I navigate what has been passed down to me, and what
doesn't belong to me at all

To the Men Because They Are

Still Hitting Us

Suvechchha Saha

Can you please be kind to us?
When will you look at us gently?
And not with the cruel beastly glare that constitutes you?
Inside the dark dungeon of humiliation, we are panting.
When will you be so kind to carve a little window here and there?
The little fish has come out from behind the convex lens
and it needs saving.

When will you please stop hitting us?
Behind all these mountains of utensil with leftover curry
and the piles of dirty clothes in the bathroom
(well, with the machines available now for the rich ones!),
behind the brain full of unsaid and said duties,
can you please look at us and see the bruises –
the bluish sores and the aching body from all your kicks and slaps
　　　and punches?

Or those dilated pupils fixed at nowhere!
Will you be able to see, if we beg you, the powerlessness of our being,
and not commemorate that discovery by hitting us more?

Can you please have mercy upon our every audacity,
because where I live, we are daring every moment – the rich and
the poor alike –
and getting beaten for that.
Will you please fuck your puny shitty existence and be damned in
hell?

What Is this Grief of Wanting More?

Rhiya Pau

Crusts of the river are burning –
at a sculpture of mourning, they serve grief.

Cast ash with soil in the bowls of our hands,
this garden we dig to observe grief.

Do not walk the swallowing quiet alone,
or alone you will learn to conserve grief.

Devotees hold hostage reservoirs of memory,
long will this thirsty cartel preserve grief.

Spin ghazals and weep, for djinns, for ghouls,
for the past stilled in ink, we reserve grief.

O infidel, deserter – begging for you,
an infant shackled to the kerb of grief.

Come home, beloved, my chamber lies empty,
what sins did we carve to deserve grief?

White

Gita Baliga-Savel

Here

In the absence of colour, in this whiteness

I find different meanings

      varied symbols

Angelic protection, purity, innocence

Or

A shroud

Death

A life sentence of mourning

      in widowhood

An edict

Be

      absent

      silent

devoid of

joy

desire

voice

Lower your head

Have

You

No

SHAME?

Shame?

No

I have no shame

I allow my body to brown

under the sun

I draw black lines on my eyelids

with kajol

Smear ochre

under my brow

Pink returns

to my cheeks

Blush creeps

up my neck

Red blood engorges

all of my extremities

As I run my fingers

across my ribs

I am resplendent

Wind, Blow on the Grass

Mashiat Zahin

O wind, blow on the grass! I'm alone like this sentence.
The weariness, so thick, that cannot haunt me
Makes me incorporeal as the night leaves.

Lying on the side of an infinite street
And millions of cranes beside –
With a leg severed,
Gray.
Boiling little houses in the desert.

The wind summons, 'Come... come...
Come...'
A little bit of her hair trembles –
The one I saw dancing like the gust –

But couldn't tell
A politeness –
With the speed of the wind
Sank into my chest.

You Carry Separation with You

S.S. Haque

remember, Pakistani? *I remember England*
ice dropping from the sky, chana-choor under my shoes
Amma's food between my toes, mother tongue a dog
licking it out; my belly was never full –
sleep a slip of time

in Stepney Green we dig for fossils
after the upset the sofa is mud; our fingers
stuck and there are worms in this tomb
our lives are a relic fusing with dinosaurs
historians losing everything of Late Antiquity

Auntie's face carved into stone… *he left to provide*
for five siblings… not enough land in the land of deltas
the air is cadaverine and crying won't solve it…
I leave a leg in the sofa; it was bruised and scarred
Abba, what are you doing here at the End of the World Party?

at the beginning of *White Teeth*
there's uncle John and the white woman
head flung back, her magazine mouth swallowing

the visa and you jump in and find her
breath perfumed, actually, like desire

later a letter flies to your ancestors
your brother cross-legged by a pond
grasps the paper bird and spills its entrails
as putrid as a story spat from a torturer's mouth

Biographies

NIKITA AASHI CHADHA   *p. 62*

Nikita is a multidisciplinary artist committed to spotlighting the 'other': a poet, singer, writer and space curator. They're an established facilitator, designing and delivering bespoke creative workshops to holding closed spaces for intersectional folks. Nikita advocates for an intersectional lens and approach – they're interested in the power of creativity and how it interconnects with identity, especially disability, race, gender and sexuality. Their work is based on lived and diasporic experience: Nikita believes that every intersectional person is a natural storyteller. Our stories are powerful and needed. We should all be confident in telling them.

ABHIJEET   *p. 57*

Abhijeet is a multilingual poet and translator based in Manchester; he is a student of Creative Writing at Manchester Metropolitan University. This is the first time his English work has been published. This particular poem is part of an ongoing project of *Lucknow Poems*, a collection paying homage to the city where he was born and raised.

MEDIAH AHMED   *p. 77*

Mediah Ahmed holds an MSci in Astrophysics and a PhD in Biophysics. She sparked her passion for theatre at Royal

Court's Muslim Unheard Voices playwriting workshops, debuting *Repentance* at ANGLE at the Bush. She has poetry published in the SALIDAA and Keats House Poets anthologies and monologues in the *Hear Me Now* anthology. Her recent theatre venture was the *Gaza Monologues* – an online solidarity event. She is currently exploring her Punjabi heritage, delving into its history and her own ancestry through connecting with the Classical Punjabi Sufi Poets and the spirituality, wisdom and philosophy embedded within their poetry.

MEV AKRAM   *p. 38*

Mev Akram was born in Rawalpindi and raised in Yorkshire. She has a degree in English and now teaches the subject in Lincolnshire. Whilst she is well acquainted with spoken word, this is her first poem in the written form. She describes writing as a cathartic experience which helps her make sense of her life's experiences as an immigrant, a feminist, a socialist and a rebel. She enjoys spending time travelling, going to gigs and being in nature.

NAILA ALI   *p. 48*

Naila is an Integrative therapist, facilitator, conference speaker, writer and artist working in private practice. She has a particular interest in identity, migration/displacement, individual, ancestral and collective trauma, women's issues with regard to autonomy, patriarchy, faith and custom/culture. She has exhibited at the Horniman Museum Tea Exhibition and performs spoken word, most recently at the Royal Albert Hall.

SAV ALTAIR HAMID   *p. 76*

Sav Altair Hamid is a graduate of the English and Creative Writing program at Royal Holloway, University of London, and an alum of the HarperCollins Author Academy. He enjoys playing with the fluidity of language beyond traditional forms in order to write against their historically exclusionary practices. Their first poetry collection, *FLOCK*, navigates connection, lineage, and identity through motifs of nature and the avian. His work has also been published by Young Writers and the Elegists Collective.

MONIZA ALVI   *p. 15*

Moniza Alvi was born in Pakistan in 1954 to an English mother and a Pakistani father. She grew up in Hertfordshire. Her first collection, *The Country at My Shoulder* (Oxford University Press, 1993), was shortlisted for the T. S. Eliot and the Whitbread poetry prizes. *Europa* (Bloodaxe, 2008) and *At the Time of Partition* (Bloodaxe, 2013) were also shortlisted for the T.S. Eliot Prize. Her most recent collection is *Fairoz* (Bloodaxe, 2022). Moniza received a Cholmondeley Award in 2002. She is a Fellow of the Royal Society of Literature.

ANSUYA   *p. 28*

Ansuya spent her formative years in India but now considers herself a Londoner. She loves expressing herself through poetry with the occasional burst of flash fiction. Her work has appeared in anthologies and publication such as *Between the Lines*, *Black in White*, *Drawn to the Light Press*, *Gypsophila*, *Half Way Down the Stairs*, *Last Stanza Journal*, *Rattle*, *Crowstep Journal* and *The Broken Spine*.

A couple of her poems were shortlisted for the Alpine and Aurora prizes in 2022. Her pamphlet *I Killed the Marriage Proposal* was highly commended by Erbacce and longlisted at Cerasus in 2024.

ANETTE APPADURAY   *p. 3*
Anette is a poet who was born and raised in Kuala Lumpur, Malaysia. She currently lives in York, England. She enjoys reading and writing poetry, spending time in nature and being astonished by the simple things in life.

LAVANYA ARORA   *p. 83*
Lavanya is an academic turned freelance researcher and writer, currently based in Bengaluru, India. They find solace in nature, cooking for their friends, and the world of Ghibli movies. Their work has previously been published in *gulmohur quarterly*, *Usawa Literary Review*, *The Phosphene Magazine*, and *TARSHI's In Plainspeak*. They are a part of the 2024 cohort of The Himalayan Emerging Writers Residency, where they will work on their first novel.

GITA BALIGA-SAVEL   *p. 101*
Gita Baliga-Savel's writing pushes boundaries with issues relating to caste, race and gender roles, while questioning constructs such as 'success' and 'shame'. When she's not happily tutoring young people, her days are filled with writing, pup walks, hikes, dancing at concerts, the occasional kayaking adventure, reading and her people. She received her MA in Educational Psychology-Counseling from the University of Nebraska-Lincoln and her BA in English from Franklin and Marshall College. Her family consists of two

sweet children, a wonderful daughter-in-law and a darling pup. She lives in San Jose, California.

KOUSHIK BANERJEA   *p. 73*

Koushik Banerjea is the author of two novels: *Another Kind of Concrete* (Jacaranda, 2020) & *Category Unknown* (London Books, 2022). His short stories have appeared in: *Salvation in Stereo, Minor Literatures, Verbal, Writers Resist, The Good Journal* and in the crime-fiction anthologies, *Shots in the Dark* and *Shots in the Dark II.* He has had poems published in *Mogadored, Razur Cuts* magazine and online in *House of Poetry* magazine. If he didn't write he'd probably lose it, which is a bit ironic as the state of the world has largely done his loaf in anyway.

ASHOK BERY   *p. 25*

Ashok Bery was born in Pune, India, and lives in London. He has taught at a number of universities and is currently a Research Associate at SOAS, University of London. His work has appeared in several anthologies and magazines, including *PN Review, Poetry Wales, The North* and *Stand.* His poem in this anthology is part of a long sequence of poetry and prose about the Indian uprising of 1857, known in Imperial historiography as the 'Indian Mutiny'.

DEVJANI BODEPUDI   *p. 40*

Devjani Bodepudi is a writer and teacher based in the UK who has been published in various anthologies and zines. Notably, Devjani was shortlisted for the Aurora Poetry Prize in 2023, and her debut poetry pamphlet, *For the Daughters Carried Here on the Hips of Their Mothers* (Fawn Press, 2023) won the Saboteur Award, also in 2023.

SELMA CARVALHO   *p. 17*

Selma Carvalho is the author of two fiction novellas, *Sisterhood of Swans* and *Notes on a Marriage*, both published by Speaking Tiger, India. She has been shortlisted in numerous short-story and poetry contests, including the London Short Story prize, and was winner of the 2018 Leicester Writes short-story prize.

RISHI DASTIDAR   *p. 72*

A poem from Rishi Dastidar's Laurel Prize-longlisted third collection, *Neptune's Projects* (Nine Arches Press), was included in *The Forward Book of Poetry 2024*. He is editor of *The Craft: A Guide to Making Poetry Happen in the 21st Century* (Nine Arches Press), and co-editor of *Too Young, Too Loud, Too Different: Poems from Malika's Poetry Kitchen* (Corsair). He also reviews poetry for *The Guardian* (UK) and is Chair of *Wasafiri*.

MANJOT DHALIWAL   *p. 93*

Manjot Dhaliwal is a British Canadian poet, researcher, writer and teacher. She is currently completing her PhD at the University of Sussex. Her research, which is inspired by her own experiences, explores South Asian women's identities and family histories through poetry. She believes in poetry's ability to facilitate storytelling and community building. As such, she is in the process of setting up a community-based poetry project, Another Story. Her own poetry explores heritage, relationships and empowerment. She hopes to publish a full collection of her poetry in the near future.

NAWSHIN FLORA   *p. 10*

Nawshin Flora is a writer and poet based in Dhaka, Bangladesh. She is currently a grad student at the University of Dhaka and a contributor at *The Daily Star*. This particular poem was written for her mother.

Z.R. GHANI   *p. 23*

Z.R. Ghani is from London. Her poems, which explore themes of identity, femininity, religion and nature, have been published in anthologies by Magma, Arachne Press and Black Bough Poetry. Her debut poetry pamphlet *In the Name of Red* (2024) is out with the Emma Press.

ANITA GOVEAS   *p. 45*

Anita Goveas is British-Asian, and fuelled by hazelnut cappuccinos and paneer jalfrezi. She was first published in the 2016 London Short Story Prize anthology, most recently by Emergent Literary, but this is the first time she's had a piece published that she intended to be a poem, and she's surprised and grateful. Her debut flash collection, *Families and Other Natural Disasters* (2020) was published by Reflex Press, and she co-edited (with Susmita Battacharya and Farhana Khalique) *Flash Fusion*, an anthology of flash fiction, writing prompts and interviews by and about authors of South Asian heritage, due to be published by Dahlia Publishing.

KINSHUK GUPTA   *p. 46*

Kinshuk Gupta is a bilingual writer, poet and translator who works at the intersection of gender, health and sexuality. His debut book of short fiction, *Yeh Dil Hai Ki Chordarwaja*, Hindi's first modern LGBT short-story collection, was published to great critical acclaim in 2023. He is the winner of prestigious awards including the India Today-Aaj Tak Sahitya Jagriti Udayiman Lekhak Samman (2023); Akhil Bhartiya Yuva Kathakar Alankaran (2022); and Dr Anamika Poetry Prize (2021). He has been shortlisted for the Toto Awards for Creative Writing (2023); The Bridport Prize (2022); Srinivas Rayparol Poetry Prize (2021); and All India Poetry Competition (2018). His work has appeared or is forthcoming in *Rattle*, *adda*, *On the Edge* (Penguin Random House, 2023), *Late-Blooming Cherries: Haiku Poets from India* (Harper Collins, 2024), among others. He has been awarded the South Asia Speaks 2023 Fellowship to work on his poetry manuscript with Tishani Doshi.

SHASTA HANIF ALI   *p. 29*

Shasta is a writer and poet. Her writing delicately navigates the legacy of race and heritage, where themes of memory and language interlace and disrupt. Shasta's writing has been published in the Association for Scottish Literature, Federation of Writers Scotland, Sidhe Press and Our Time Is a Garden Anthology (IASH), among others. Recently Shasta was nominated as one of Edinburgh's 100 trailblazing women past and present, and honoured in a mural, which was exhibited across Edinburgh.

S.S. HAQUE   *p. 105*

S.S. Haque is a British Bangladeshi poet and novelist. She has performed at poetry nights across London and published poetry and short fiction in literary journals for nearly a decade. She holds a master's in creative writing from the University of Oxford.

HUMUS   *p. 66*

Humus is a multifaceted soul, creating art of both written and visual expression. She dips her brush into the art of poetry, singing, digital art and martial arts. She started her spoken-word journey after the coronavirus lockdown, when she faced disownment from her family, and channelled her emotions into her poetry. Her writing captures the nuances of life's journey, from the joys of love to the ache of loss. With a relatable and profound writing style, she crafts verse that finds a home in the hearts of her audience. One of her most popular pieces, 'I Like a Man', a playful yet real exploration of love and desire, has garnered over three million views across Instagram and TikTok. Merging poetry and digital art, she crafts custom illustrations and garments for the spoken-word community, translating the thoughts of poets and artists into visual stories that leave a lasting impression.

MADRI KALUGALA   *p. 53*

Madri Kalugala is the author of three collections of poetry, *An Almond Moon and the White Owl* (2016), *Exulansis* (2021) and *Songs for Constance* (2024). She has had her poems and short stories published in various anthologies, most recently *Out of Sri Lanka* (Bloodaxe, 2023), and is currently experimenting with mixed-genre forms and non-fiction. She has grown up in Brunei and Sri Lanka, and writes as a way to unravel and understand the complications of human existence. She loves to paint, make art, go for long walks in the woods and spend time contemplating nature and nothingness.

THIRD SPACE

JAYANT KASHYAP   *p. 18*

Jayant Kashyap is a writer and artist based in India. He
has published two pamphlets, *Survival* (*Clare Songbirds*,
2019) and *Unaccomplished Cities* (*Ghost City Press*, 2020), and
a zine, *Water* (*Skear Zines*, 2021). His poems have appeared
in *POETRY*, *Magma*, *Arc*, *Acumen* and *Poetry Wales*, among
others, and has received honourable mentions in Atlanta
Review's *Dan Veach Prize for Younger Poets* in 2021 and 23. Jayant
was shortlisted for the Poetry Business *New Poets Prize* in 2021
and 22, and was nominated for the Pushcart Prize in 2018
and for Sundress Publications' *Best of the Net* in 2022 and 23.

RUPINDER KAUR WARAICH   *p. 88*

Rupinder Kaur Waraich is a multidisciplinary artist based in
Birmingham. Her work often looks at the linguistic intersection
of the body, language, history, sexuality and spirituality through
the feminine narrative and gaze. She explores different artistic
disciplines from poetry, writing, performing and acting. Her
debut poetry book Rooh (2018) was published with Verve
Poetry Press; she is currently working on her second collection.

EMMETT MEHABOOB   *p. 95*

Emmett Mehaboob (he/him) is an Indian transgender writer
born and raised in Kerala and Saudi Arabia. He is inspired
by nature, religion and parasocial relationships with pop
divas, which are really all the same thing. He is currently
working on a master's in countering online extremism. Poetry
provides necessary levity, alongside parenting a very grumpy
old cat. He has previously been featured in the *Resonance*
anthology, and his work with the collective *Poets for Palestine*
has fundraised for NGOs and university encampments.

A.A. MALIK   *p. 20*

A.A. Malik is an established writer of fiction and non-fiction, published in a range of media. An emerging (once, initially reluctant) poet, her poetry can be found in anthologies and journals exploring the themes of spirituality, motherhood and the aspects of identity that are influenced by ancestral, ethnic and childhood experiences, with a focus on dual/multi belonging. She holds a Creative Writing diploma from the University of Oxford. When not writing she can usually be found drinking (and spilling) tea, deciphering hieroglyphs or sweeping legs in a dojo.

JASPREET MANDER   *p. 79*

Having taught English literature and language to postgraduates and supervised research at Punjabi University, Patiala (Punjab) India, Jaspreet Mander moved to England in 2021. She completed MA (Creative Writing) at Leeds Trinity University in 2022. Her poetry and prose have been published in *Dream Catcher*, *Shine*, Wordspace anthologies and *Hear Me Now* (Methuen, 2022), and she has made programmes as a part of Chapel FM's *Writing On Air* 2022 and 2023 radio festivals.

JAY MITRA   *p. 64*

Jay Mitra is a punk poet and non-fiction writer based in London. Born in India but raised in Yorkshire, they have spent their life melding two cultures into one five-foot body. Jay was one of the winners of the Creative Future Writers' Awards 2023 and is one of Apples and Snakes' 40 Future Voices in Poetry. They have featured on BBC Radio 3 and BBC Radio 6, and in a variety of festivals including BBC's Contains

Strong Language, Manchester Pride and Manchester Punk Festival. Currently, Jay is pursuing a career in teaching and working as a freelance writer and facilitator.

JAWEERYA MOHAMMAD   *p. 8*

Jaweerya Mohammad is a passionate educator, having taught Middle School English for many years. Her writing is shaped by her Muslim and first-generation Pakistani American identity. She has a poem forthcoming in House of Amal's anthology on Palestine. She firmly believes in the power of words, and that storytelling can foster a more empathetic and just world.

ANITA NAHAL   *p. 32*

Anita Nahal, Ph.D., is an Indian American author-academic. Nominated twice for the Pushcart Prize (2022 and 23) and a finalist for the Tagore Literary Prize (2023), Anita has one novel, four poetry collections and four books for children published, and has edited five poetry anthologies. Anita's poems have been anthologised in over twenty international anthologies, and hundreds have been published in journals in the US, Asia and Australia. Her third book of poetry, *What's Wrong with Us Kali Women?*, is prescribed as mandatory reading at Utrecht University. She teaches at the University of the District of Columbia, Washington DC.

HANA ORMARA   *p. 34*

Hana Ormara is a British poet whose first work was published in an anthology by the International Human Rights Arts Movement (IHRAM) in 2023. She holds a degree in Industrial Design from Central Saint Martins and has completed postgraduate studies in History of Art, specialising in postcolonial theory. Her writing is deeply inspired by her Baloch heritage and its indigenous traditions of poetry and storytelling through spoken word. Hana draws on themes of displacement, womanhood and identity seen through a lens of diaspora and a love of humanity. In a world where humans are becoming increasingly dependent on technology and artificial intelligence, Hana believes our survival and evolution relies on voicing the space between our hearts and minds. Her aim is to share the spirit of human experience through poetic word.

SUCHITA PARIKH-MUNDUL   *p. 42*

Suchita Parikh-Mundul works as a writer and copy editor in Mumbai, India, and many of her articles have been published by *The Swaddle*. Her poetry has appeared in literary magazines like *The Bombay Literary Magazine*, Sahitya Akademi's *Indian Literature*, *Usawa Literary Review* and *Outlook India*, as well as in national and international anthologies.

RHIYA PAU   *p. 100*

Rhiya Pau's debut collection, *Routes* (Arachne Press, 2022) won an Eric Gregory Award from the Society of Authors and commemorates fifty years since her family arrived in the UK, chronicling the migratory history of her ancestors and navigating the conflicts of identity that arise within the East African-Indian diaspora. Rhiya won the Creative Future Writers' Award in 2021 and her poem 'Salutation' was highly commended in the 2023 Forward Prize. She is one half of the ORIGINS Poetry Duo, who write and perform collective poetry that does away with 'ownership' and 'linearity' to decentralise and decolonise the traditional project of history.

KARI PINDORIA *p. 16*

Kari Pindoria is a poet and writer from north-west London. Her writing appears in *And Other Poems, Propel, Ink, Sweat and Tears, Unbroken Journal* and various anthologies, such as *Tales from the Kitchen* and *Chicken + Bread Zine*. She often daydreams about living in a Studio Ghibli film and being taller.

CLARE RAMSARAN *p. 51*

Clare Ramsaran is a writer of Indo-Guyanese/Irish heritage, and holds a master's degree in Creative Writing (University of San Francisco). Her writing has been published in Britain and the US, and she was delighted to read her poetry at the renowned City Lights Bookstore in San Francisco. Clare's novel manuscript *Kala Polari* was longlisted for the 2022 SI Leeds Prize, and she was the winner of the 2023 Book Edit Writers Prize and shortlisted for Unbound Firsts Prize (2024–25). Clare has worked in human rights education, for the Mayor of London (Ken, not Boris) and as a technology trainer in Silicon Valley and Manchester.

PRIYANKA SACHETI *p. 85*

Priyanka Sacheti is a writer, poet, and photographer based in Bangalore, India. She was raised in the Sultanate of Oman and educated at the universities of Warwick and Oxford. She's published widely about art, gender and culture in international digital and print publications. Her literary work and art has appeared in many journals like *Barren, Dust Mag Poetry, Common, Parentheses Art, Popshot,*

The Lunchticket and *The Selkie*, as well as various poetry and fiction anthologies, such as *Yearbook of Indian Poetry in English 2022* and *Botanical Short Stories*. One of her short stories was recently nominated for Best of Net. She's Visual Narratives editor at *Usawa Literary Review*; she's also currently working on book-length poetry and fiction works.

SUVECHCHHA SAHA   *p. 98*

Suvechchha Saha is a reader and writer. Her short stories have been published previously and currently she is writing her first novel. One other thing that she is in love with is the moor from the window of Wuthering Heights.

ANKITA SAXENA   *p. 44*

Ankita Saxena is a British-Indian writer and performer. Her debut poetry collection, *Mother | Line*, was published by Verve Poetry Press in April 2023. She is a former Barbican Young Poet, Foyle Young Poet, Octavia poet and one half of the poetry duo ORIGINS. Her poetry is published in *Wasafiri*, *Modern Poetry in Translation* and *Bath Magg*, and her fiction is published in *Brown Girl Magazine* and *Gutter Street*. She read English at Oxford and currently works for a not-for-profit organisation which seeks to improve outcomes for the most excluded communities in the UK.

SNEHA SUBRAMANIAN KANTA   *p. 14*

Sneha Subramanian Kanta is an academician and award-winning writer currently residing in Mississauga, Ontario. She is the author of five chapbooks, including *Ancestral-Wing* (Porkbelly Press, 2024), *Every Elegy Is a Love Poem* (Variant Lit, 2024) and *Ghost Tracks* (Louisiana Literature,

2020). Her work has been supported by several institutions including Ontario Arts Council, Tin House, the Charles Wallace Trust, the Vijay Nambisan Foundation and Rutgers University. Her multi-genre work has been published in *Prairie Schooner*, *Shenandoah*, *West Branch* and elsewhere. She is one of the founding editors of *Parentheses Journal*.

LAILA SUMPTON   *p. 6*

Laila Sumpton is a poet, editor, performer and educator who works with schools, hospitals, museums, galleries and charities on a wide variety of poetry projects. She co-founded the arts and education organisation Poetry Vs Colonialism and is an associate artist with intergenerational charity Magic Me. Laila co-edited *Where We Find Ourselves* (2021), an anthology by Global Majority writers published by Arachne Press with fellow poet Sandra A. Agard. She has been commissioned by Tate Modern, Poet in the City, the Tower of London and the Royal Free Hospital, amongst others, and has been published in numerous anthologies and magazines including *Ambit* and *Modern Poetry in Translation*.

TEHNUKA   *p. 89*

Tehnuka is an Eelam Tamil writer from Aotearoa New Zealand who calls upon you, dear reader, to join her in refusing and resisting the genocide of Palestinian people and the colonisation of Palestine. Resist with every breath and deed until Palestine is free – until we are all free.

ILISHA THIRU PURCELL   *p. 12*

Ilisha Thiru Purcell is an award-winning poet from Newcastle upon Tyne. She is part of the inaugural Poets of Colour

Incubator Programme and was a Young Creative Associate with New Writing North, where she created a poetry film inspired by classical Tamil love poetry, akam poetry. Her work has appeared in publications such as *Butcher's Dog* and *Bi+ Lines Anthology* and she was shortlisted for Nine Arches' *Primers Volume 7*. She is a member of Brown Girls Write.

ANANNYA UBEROI   *p. 30*

Anannya Uberoi was born in Delhi, and now lives in Madrid. She is poetry editor at *The Bookends Review*, the winner of the sixth Singapore Poetry Contest, and a Pushcart Prize nominee. Through her writing, Uberoi explores themes of identity, displacement, and the limits of language in articulating human-nature connectedness. Her work has appeared in *Poetry Wales*, *The Emerson Review* and *Poetry Salzburg Review*.

VIJAYA VENKATESAN   *p. 70*

Born and raised in India, Vijaya Venkatesan went to university in the UK. She has an LL.M in International Law from Cambridge University and has spent most of her professional life in the public sector. She has been longlisted for the National Poetry Competition, shortlisted for the Bridport Prize and published in Renard Press's anthology *Kinship: Poems Exploring Belonging*. She lives in London with an unkempt garden and an eccentric wire-haired dachshund.

KATHLEEN WENADEN   *p. 4*

Kathleen Wenaden currently lives in Wivenhoe, Essex and is of Sri Lankan heritage. She is gradually making her life more spacious and describes herself as a mother, medic, pilgrim and poet. She has had writing published in local anthologies, and in online publications *Fevers of the Mind* and *TORCH: A Digital Anthology of Home* (Oxford University). She has had several publications in *British Journal of General Practice Life* (2023). She is also co-lead of the RCGP Specialist Interest Group in Creative Health, and is particularly interested in the portals between art and health.

RISHIKA WILLIAMS   *p. 59*

Rishika Williams is a poet and performer born in Nigeria, living in London. She is of Indian origin. Both her parents' families left Hyderabad, Sind during the partition of India. She is predominantly a narrative poet in the long form who writes about violence against women and girls (VAWG). She has performed at survivor events, The Brighton Dome, NYC, London open mics and on Indian digital platforms. An excerpt from her book-length poem was published in *Between the Lines Anthology 2022* and two new forms of hers were published in a pamphlet on the Poetry School blog, *Form Lab*. She was shortlisted for the Malorie Blackman Scholarship 2022 and long listed for the National Poetry Competition 2023.

MASHIAT ZAHIN   *p. 104*

Mashiat Zahin lives in Bangladesh. She is a poet and a communist. Her obsession with the bridge and contrast of the collective and the personal keeps her writing. Through writing she permits herself to explore the psychological reality freely and expect people to meet in the untold between the syntax and devices. She has a book called *The Contrast of the Story of a Bird Than the Flock* in her mother tongue Bangla.

Index of First Lines

Acknowledgements

I would first like to thank Arts Council England – this project would not exist without their generous funding. I also want to thank my mother, who sadly died in April 2024, but was my greatest supporter and biggest fan. She was twice displaced – first by the 1947 Partition of India, and then by coming here, but she just got on with whatever life threw at her. Her family meant everything to her, and she always put us first.

A massive thank you goes to Will Dady-Leonard. As soon as I told him about the Third Space project, he said, 'I'm in – what can I do?' His support, for the anthology and wider project, during one of the most difficult periods of my life, has kept me going.

Next, a big thank you to Lewis Biggs, my mentor, with whom I had the healing conversation which led to me writing poetry again. He is kind, funny and honest. And thanks too to Professor Partha Mitter, whose work I discovered during my MFA. He has read all my poems, encouraged me to keep writing, and offered many valuable insights into culture and identity.

I also want to thank the amazing judges, Farhana Shaikh, Gita Raleigh, Navkiran Kaur Mann and Reshma Ruia, who took on the difficult task of selecting fifty poems from over two hundred – and, of course, all the poets who submitted their precious work.

I am also grateful to Nikita Chadha and Rhiya Pau for their regular messages checking on me and reminding me to take care of myself.

Thanks also to Jane Commane of Nine Arches Press and Zoe Brigley of Poetry Wales for their enthusiasm for the project, and for helping to spread the word.

Lastly, I want to thank David, Safia and Amalia, my family, whose love and pride in my work means the world to me.

A NOTE ON SUSTAINABILITY

RENARD PRESS feels strongly that there is no denying the climate crisis, and we all have a part to play in fixing the problem.

We are proud to be one of the UK's first climate-positive publishers, taking more carbon out of the air than we put in. How? We reduce our emissions as much as possible, using green energy, printing locally and choosing the materials we use carefully; we calculate our carbon footprint and doubly offset it through gold-standard schemes; and we plant a tree for every order we receive via our website to give back to the planet.

Find out more at:

RENARDPRESS.COM/ECO